KU-051-871

LEEDS COL OF ART & DESIGN
R56128J0084

JOHANNA BILLING

I'M LOST WITHOUT YOUR RHYTHM

CAMDEN ARTS CENTRE, LONDON MODERN ART OXFORD ARNOLFINI, BRISTOL

III 3 artists 3 spaces 3 years

CONTENTS

INTRODUCTION

Over the last decade Johanna Billing's videos have reflected on routine, rehearsal and ritual. Through a deft observational style, she places subtle emphasis on both the fragility of individual performance and the power of collective experience. Billing herself has also said that she is obsessed by circularity and retrospection.

Billing's new video work *I'm Lost Without Your Rhythm* (2009), is based around the recording of a dance choreography workshop in Iasi, Romania. Led by Swedish choreographer Anna Vnuk, with whom Billing last worked over a decade ago, there is no final performance as such. Instead the resulting video links several days' activity into a continuous process of live improvisation between choreographer, dancers and local musicians which was originally watched by an audience who were free to come and go as they pleased.

For Billing, the project was an attempt to explore, along with the participating individuals and audience, what contemporary dance can be, or means today, especially in relation to a developing country and economy such as Romania. The work becomes about movement in general and choreography coming closer to everyday life than might at first be imagined.

Ever since her video *Graduate Show* (1999) in which Billing's contemporaries at art school danced to a 1980s soundtrack, music, sound and rhythm have woven a continuous thread through her video works. Even *Project for a Revolution* (2000), though without a musical score, has rhythm at its heart, with ambient sounds of a regurgitating photocopier and the restless rustle of young people apparently waiting around for something to happen.

Young people have frequently become a focus of her camera's 'eye', despite each work having hugely divergent contexts and content as their premise. The methodologies Billing employs turn film making into projects where the participants are an intrinsic part of their process. So not only the dancers, actors and audience constitute the participants for

I'm Lost Without Your Rhythm but also the musicians, percussionists, a marimba and piano player, as well as film crew, sound technician and stills photographer.

These constituent parts of Billing's videos – their people, locations, activities, recording, editing and sounds – come together in a lengthy post-production process, making the whole not only greater than the sum of the individual parts but far from the original course or trajectory the project set out upon. Billing acknowledges that her editing is approached in an often rhythmical way itself – just as music can convey atmosphere, so can the nature of the edit. She exploits these editorial 'cuts' and the bits in-between, those that you cannot see, but feel. [1]

Like many of her contemporaries, Billing's interests are wide, taking in philosophy, music and social science as well as influence from her artist-friends' practices. In the past, Johanna's work has been acknowledged as being imbued with an appreciation of her native Sweden's recent history and in particular the failure of her generation to connect with politics and the importance of social democracy in the same way that her parents' generation had. It is this co-joining of the political with the collaborative that often results in her work being defined as 'participative'. In fact, as the accompanying interview with Iasi-based writer Cristian Nae illustrates, who also witnessed the 'performance' she created for the Biennial, she is more often than not creating an open structure in which people function in a way that is much more democratic. Billing stages situations where something may or may not take place. Her skill lies in combining the choreography of the individuals whose trust she earns with facilitating their freedom to perform naturally, bringing the whole together through her clever editing. The subsequently unfolding dramas hold the viewer enthralled, and not infrequently moved. Perhaps the possibility of watching people fail, or struggling to do something not entirely natural to them, whether it be singing in a foreign language in *Magical World* (2005), contemplating a high dive in

Where She Is At (2001), or learning to sail in *This Is How We Walk On The Moon* (2007), is a cathartic experience in itself. Either way, Johanna Billing brings a unique perspective to, and forges an emotional connection with, the viewers of her films because of the investment she makes in the people who feature in them. Certainly there is never one particular 'group' as such that she works with; indeed Billing has said that she would like to expand further on what we mean by collectively gathering people and defining them in this way, as institutions often gently encourage artists to do, whether by gender, nationality, their shared interests or the fact they simply take the same bus to work. Perhaps as she has intimated herself, the most interesting place to occupy as a 'participant' is that space between the collective experience of producing an art work and the private experience of seeing it in the context of an art gallery or cinema.

As well as music often being a central part of the atmosphere of her videos, Billing is also involved with music production, running an independent music label *Make It Happen* which releases records and organises concerts. So appropriately, if a 'coda' defines the concluding passage or movement of a piece of music, then this publication, more programme than catalogue, functions similarly for *I'm Lost Without Your Rhythm*.

1 Johanna Billing, *Look Behind Us A Blue Sky*, 2007, Carole Bertinet, 'Editing Is Musical', pp114-115

BRUCE HAINES

I'M LOST WITHOUT
YOUR RHYTHM
A PROJECT BY
JOHANNA BILLING
LIVE WORKSHOP &
FILM RECORDING
I'M LOST
YOUR

Cristian Nae: *The concept of community is often linked to your artistic practice. I think of 'community' as fundamentally an open, fragile, incomplete, and temporary social phenomenon - existentially groundless. What does it mean for you?*

Johanna Billing: The word has so many different meanings: geographically and ecologically, or in terms of activities, identities or shared values or interests. I wouldn't know how to pick one simple way to describe it. I have to say though, that I actually rarely work with pre-existing communities or groups in society. On the contrary, the people that take part often come from various different places, groups, belief systems, ideas, or backgrounds. The films are not attempts to portray certain groups or communities, but rather situations made up of a collective of temporarily joined individuals. It is the differences between them that I am interested in, and the fact that normally they would not be in this specific made-up situation.

What makes you choose or propose a specific, particular setting for an action?

Often, it is an intuitive process that has its starting point in dreams, memories or feelings I may have been puzzled by. So, in a sense, it can be a very psychological process in which things get triggered or emphasised by meeting certain people or being in a specific surrounding. Many times it is about tracing something back, trying to find out the reason why some situations, images and thoughts get stuck in my head and are difficult to pin down with words and understand on a more conscious level.

Does your chosen situation or context start as a theme, or is it the result of an intuitive process?

In the beginning, there is seldom one specific theme. The contexts of the films are the result of a process where I am trying to deal with situations I find myself in more accidentally. Of course I make a lot of choices on the way all the time but I don't sit at home making the script and choosing a location. The location triggers the idea to begin with, and the more I work on something, the more it expands and becomes multilayered.

Are these performative processes you frame a sort of laboratory for living in a common situation? Could they be extended allegorically to the conceptual, contextual relations of everyday existence, which one could see as the message of your works? A laboratory where individuals are discovering themselves when confronted by a specific, collective task?

Yes, I guess you could describe it like that, and it is certainly about process and finding something on the way. However, while many of the projects have almost a catalyst function that way, I try to avoid using words like laboratory, as I am always very concerned that the projects are never about using people to conduct experiments. Instead, the set up is improvised and experimental, and the participants are very much a part of controlling the output and the result.

Sometimes you work as director, choreographer, and producer of a collective performance. What is the importance of involving a group of people in producing the work?

The works themselves are never *about* the community or the group as a theme, I am much more interested in documenting the individual. But somehow, working with several people at the same time actually makes it easier to get close to that. The groups are somehow representative of some kind of backdrop, a society that is centered around the individual. Interestingly enough though, my experience is that just by showing a group making something together, no matter if it is a way of organising or just about being, often this becomes a focus for people because it seems quite a powerful and odd looking image or constellation itself in today's society, which has become so individualistic.

Music plays a major part in your video works. Why do you emphasise it as a specific artistic language, especially in relation to the visual one?

Early on I started out working with staged situations, mostly using photography as a medium. But when it came to portraying atmospheres, which was what I was mostly after, I realised that working with sound was one of the most efficient tools to use. Although it is not always treated as such in visual art, to me video actually consists of half video, half sound. It has become natural for me to treat everyday, atmospheric sound – the soundscape – and music equally.

I have also been working with music parallel to art since I was a teenager, doing everything from organising concerts to writing about and producing music. So I would say many of my reasons for working with music come from the experiences I have from being such an intense listener to it. And I believe that if you can activate the 'listening' more in the viewer while they look at the film, you can get closer to an intimate communication, as we sometimes deal with and interpret the things we see and hear on different levels. This is especially interesting to explore in exhibitions where the focus is on 'seeing'.

What does dialogue mean for you? In your films, it is mostly based on silence, or non-verbal elements like singing or dancing. These bodily actions suggest a complex and tacitly choreographed background.

I think the way the films lack dialogue and are about people expressing things in a non-verbal way is often the result of documenting people who are busy doing something, or even just thinking. There is a kind of concentration that comes out of just being present in the situation. And in that situation I guess I am putting a lot of focus on the small details, gestures, and movements that can become quite physical. And the fact that the films try to deal with things we cannot put words to can – more than other types of film genres – make their set up resemble a choreography of sorts. So, to work more directly and hands on with movement and choreography now is very challenging. I would say it is a lot about rhythm. And even if these films without dialogue or music are quite silent, they are still quite rhythmical, creating a physical dimension that in the end makes them as musical as my films with more conventional musical soundtracks.

You often produce a 'participative' situation in a very specific way. In your latest work, you involved a group of dancers as well as a 'spectator' element – the gaze of the public. How do you regard this participative element?

My experience is that it can actually sometimes be a bit confusing to talk too much about them being 'participatory' projects, as there are often certain expectations about what the outcome should be for people taking part. Personally I can relate my work to a more traditional way of working with filmmaking, when you have a kind of unquestionable collaboration with people that take part in front of the camera. There is a natural collaboration going on, and often filmmakers also work with non-actors. So this way of working with other people is not something that I feel I need to put a specific focus on.

As I also work a lot with improvisation and with situations that people are new to, there can be quite an intimate atmosphere going on, and normally in my work, these recording situations – even though they are often of performative character - are very private. Alongside this, I have worked with one-off live events. This time I was interested in bringing these two, sometimes separate, ways of working together – bringing in an audience and their view from the beginning. At the same time I wanted to make something that could be treated as two separate occasions and a film that did not necessarily have to end up as a documentation of an event.

What about dancing? What did you look for in the choreography workshop that was the starting point for your new film?

It might come down to the curiosity I have for the ways we select and sort out our experiences in different fields. What we consciously regard as an intellectual activity - verbal or physical – and what can be expressed and how. Often I think I am after a way of communicating – sometimes perhaps with oneself – that we have lost contact with. To go after a more physical way of expressing things could be a way to get closer to these kinds of things that are lying a bit hidden within us.

Does this work have any sort of contextual significance to Iasi or to the present day social situation in Romania?

I had a lot of starting points based on observations I made during my visit to Iasi, but I am still in the middle of the process of making the work, so it is difficult to know yet what meaning some of the things will have.

I knew I wanted to explore something more hands on in choreography, and also that I wanted to collaborate again with the choreographer Anna Vnuk with whom I worked ten years ago, in one of my first films which was a dance video. When first coming to Iasi I was curious about the local scene in contemporary dance. Not only did it hardly exist just then, considering Iasi is such a vibrant student city with so much cultural heritage, but there were few opportunities for people to enter this field, unless you started out as a classical ballet student at five years old. Somehow this conservative way of looking at contemporary dance became an important starting point – particularly the view of who could have access to these things. And for me, working together with this group of students (some coming from one of the few existing dance schools for amateurs as well as a group of acting students), this became an interesting place to explore ideas about what contemporary choreography could be or mean for people today. And perhaps this does not have to be specifically only about Iasi, but also about a general approach to these questions.

Who is the individual 'I', in the title of I'm Lost Without Your Rhythm *and what type of loss do you have in mind?*

The title comes from a phrase in the refrain of the song *My Heart* originally written and performed by the Swedish drum and vocal duo 'Wildbirds and Peacedrums'. I was listening to it while planning the project, and even though the lyrics are quite simple, it still took me a while to understand that the 'you' when Mariam Wallentin, the vocalist, sings *I'm Lost Without Your Rhythm* refers to her own heart and its beating. At the same time her co-musicians on the drums include her husband who she is, in the song and in other ways, also dependent on. So for me, it is both about the 'I', and about something inside us that we need to be in contact with. Secondly, we are dependent on the people around us. The song was an inspiration, particularly in the way this group based its music on similar rhythmical instruments that the live musicians in the workshop used – such as various percussion instruments and a marimba. Later on, it became interesting the way the lyrics connected to the activities that go on. The whole sentence is actually 'don't run, I am lost without your rhythm'. There is a lot of running and a continuous increasing of tempo going on in the film. This has, of course, many meanings.

While making the film, the financial crisis was becoming more and more real. I was reading about how in a situation of crisis the natural thing for humans to do is to run; and how people on different levels in society – from big companies to individuals – were continuously encouraged from all kinds of directions to keep on running as a solution to their problems. But it is not something we do only temporarily. More and more, we are turning, or using this the bodily habit of handling a crisis, into a situation where the fast speed tempo suddenly becomes the normal, everyday pace. With this rhythm one could eventually find oneself in a constant crisis. So this became another aspect of movement that was interesting to think about in relation to the choreography of the 'everyday'.

The choreography included various simple tasks for people to relate to. Was there any particular reason for choosing or proposing them?

We wanted to work with very basic movements, not so much dance-related but everyday activities. The project avoided choreographic traditions and instead tried to make something that would challenge pre-existing ideas about what contemporary choreography is. By doing this, we realised we couldn't avoid crossing other people's paths in history, choreographers such as Trisha Brown or Yvonne Rainer, who also examined the very basics of everyday movement.

I had one of the scenes planned, the collective typewriting session (on 1970s and 1980s typewriters) that gradually moves from writing to rhythm in the way the drums are eventually taking over and the participants develop a more physical activity. This was also an attempt to try to work with something that would not represent something other than what it was, almost on a physical level. These typewriters turned out to have quite a specific resonance in Romania, as during the 1980s the government regulated who could own a typewriter, which had to be registered by the police. Perhaps this was one of the reasons I could hardly find any machines from this period, and instead had to bring a couple of them over from Sweden. This background ended up becoming interesting as one of the themes in the project has been to deal with the question of who can have access to certain things in life and culture.

What is the relationship between movement and narration in your film? How does your video editing relate back to the movements of the dancers, the multiple cameras involved in recording, and the resulting multiple points of view?

Before starting the project I was thinking a lot about what happens when choreography is filmed. It immediately becomes another, or even several other choreographies, depending on the angles and the cameras. This was also something that Anna was aware of. We decided to start by creating something that was totally fragmented to begin with. Something that can be treated as just bits and pieces to pick and build something new from. So, in a way, a final choreography has never existed – not even in the live event. All exercises were made as fragments. People had to create something themselves from what they saw when they came and went during the three days. In the editing process, I treat all the material as new movements from which I am creating another choreography, based on Anna's original and the preparations around it. Although the attempt was not to create a document of the live performance, but instead something more abstract, the film actually does have a similarity to what was actually happening, as the event itself was constructed as various almost isolated situations.

Is there anything you think might also be lost from the 'live' experience of the workshop to its representation on video?

Oh, everything is lost I think. The live event was altogether a totally different thing. But that was also somehow the whole point. The presence and tension when people from outside entered the room, breaking into the semi private sphere of the big hallway we used as our 'stage' not normally used for these things, was and can never be represented. Also very little of the live musical soundtrack could be used in the film for several technical and editing reasons. For this new structure, as the film in itself is, I decided to instead make another soundtrack, going back to the inspiration of the 'Wildbirds and Peacedrums' song again, making a cover version with several vocals and percussion instruments.

Rehearsal itself seems to be a recurrent artistic motif of yours; why is this?

This project might look like a rehearsal but I was interested in the fact that we actually did not rehearse. The event was a learning situation, a performance for a live event for an audience. Since it did not lead up to anything else than what it was, there is not a before or an after, only a present. This could be the very definition of improvisation, which was perhaps the core of the whole project. I guess I am fascinated by the potential in these open-ended situations: the challenge of something remaining unfinished or unresolved.

CRISTIAN NAE is an art critic and theoretician based in Iasi, Romania.

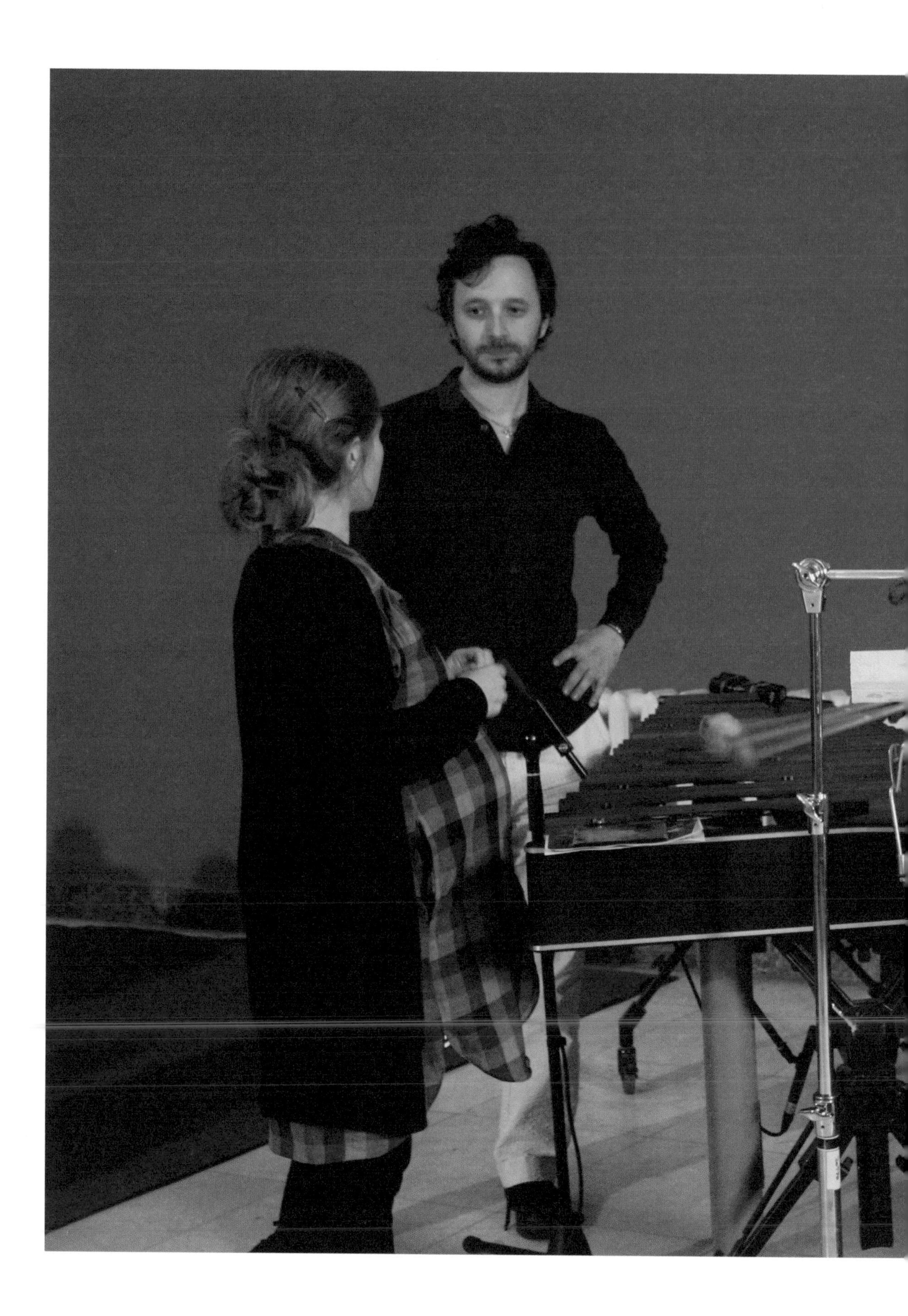

ROZAR
ALPINISM UTILITAR

IASI, ROMANIA, OCTOBER 2008

Through the wide open doors of a student house facing a large square in the centre of Iasi, passers-by could catch a glimpse of an unusual phenomenon during a week in October. This place, with connotations of 'youth' and the rhetoric of 'future generations' (suggesting learning and becoming), is in fact an ancient communist building now open to the public. In a sort of metonymic reference, the history of the edifice and its present-day gesture suggest a state of perpetual transformation undergone by Romanian society in the last twenty years and the rhetoric of change accompanying them.

A row of stairs in front of these rarely used entrance doors make this space look like an enormous theatrical scene, although not many people actually stop to take a look at what happens inside it. At the end of a long corridor on the first floor, a group of amateur dancers and theatre students from Iasi were taking part in a choreography workshop. They were gathered together on an improvised 'stage', half-way between a shooting-range and a rehearsal room. The workshop was produced with the help of a group of musicians and a professional choreographer, and it was recorded with the help of three cameras moving around the scene. By using their bodies, their movements and gestures, the dancers were learning to coordinate their actions, confronted by a series of specific, ordinary situations. At the same time, they were able to express themselves as individuals.

Few passers-by were aware that this 'rehearsal' stood for Johanna Billing's contribution to the *Periferic 8: Art as Gift* contemporary art biennial taking place in the city.

This was not the first time Billing had proposed a collaborative work involving non professional groups of people gathered together voluntarily in a rehearsal situation. Moreover, it is a manner of working which raises questions about the representation of community and its relationship with the individual. The use of amateurs challenged the relationship between staging a 'social body' and spontaneous communication among individuals. Being a 'rehearsal' stressed the incomplete and dynamic character of this social phenomenon, closer to a 'work-in-progress' and suggesting a never ending task.

It may also be worth noting that the workshop, by its choreographic and therefore performative nature, was, through its location, set against a particular historical background. During the communist regime, many artists tried to achieve individualism by means of performance – regarded as individual resistance to ideological pressure. However, this was mainly a private exercise, often performed in the intimacy of one's own home or in other, non-institutionalised and publicly unacknowledged, places. The individual's body was regarded as the ultimate battle-ground for the exercise of power and control from the totalitarian regime. Choreography was mainly used in mass festivities, specific to communist times, which involved thousands of anonymous people gathered together in order to perform the megalomaniac dreams of that delirious social machinery. In this historical context, to enact a choreographic exercise today also meant, in an oblique way, to invite an audience to a collective exercise of recollection and to suggest a test of societal cohesion for the participating individuals in this situation.

But its location and character also related to present-day Romanian society, marked by collective uncertainty about the future. Using non-professional dancers assured the authenticity of the workshop and avoided the possibility of a 'mannered' artistic expression. In Romanian society, choreography is still an under-represented profession – a situation shared by many other collective artistic practices. Therefore, even if unintended, by focusing on rhythm and mutual coordination, the workshop implicitly questioned the present-day blurred reference points of young Romanian groups. It also highlighted their fragile collective cohesion in a society characterised by a recently emerged ideology of 'change' and 'Europeanisation'.
Besides the fascinating poetics of the performance and the deeply emotional

character of the music which accompanied the experience, perhaps it is this uncomfortable but necessary self-questioning of what a collective performance means and how we adapt to changing social conditions that Billing brought as a 'gift' to the local context of Iasi and its social self-representations. But the anonymity of the dancers involved in the situation created by Billing means the event defies any particular narrative and easy categorisation.

CHRISTIAN NAE

AFTERWORD

Johanna Billing's new work, *I'm Lost Without Your Rhythm* (2009), has been produced as the second in a series of three new commissions organised by Camden Arts Centre, London; Modern Art Oxford and Arnolfini, Bristol.

The 3 Series is a three year programme which binds three, like-minded, public institutions who share a strong commitment to nurturing artists' work and ideas.

Our collective desire for the series is to enable three distinctive international artists, to create a new work and present it in three different cities. Each of the commissioned works will be gifted to a regional public collection, contributing to the development of those collections and ensuring a legacy for the artists' work in this country.

Mircea Cantor was the first artist to be commissioned. His installation, *The Need for Uncertainty*, was produced and presented in Oxford, Bristol and London throughout 2008/09. One of his works has now been presented, via the Contemporary Art Society, to the Towner Collection, Eastbourne. Following Johanna Billing, Los Angeles based filmmaker Kerry Tribe will complete the series with a project to be launched at Arnolfini in 2010.

These artists were invited after periods of research and discussion between our curatorial teams; each was felt to be at a point where they would take full advantage of the time and resources available to extend their own limits.

Johanna Billing accepted the commission at a time when her reputation and influence as an artist has become more widely established. She has wholeheartedly embraced the opportunity that was offered and we very much appreciate her hard work and commitment to creating her new work and to the production of this catalogue. Our thanks go to her and to Cristian Nae for recounting his time spent with Johanna during her filming in Iasi and for illuminating the process through the interview with her. We are thankful to Lisa Panting and Malin

Ståhl of Hollybush Gardens who represents Johanna's work in London, and Simon Josebury who has designed the format of all the 3 Series publications. He has produced a book which captures wonderfully the spirit of Johanna's project. We join Johanna in thanking all those who took part in *I'm Lost Without Your Rhythm* and assisted in the making of the work in Romania and Sweden.

Bruce Haines, Anne-Marie Watson and Richard Gough at Camden Arts Centre have worked closely with Johanna to assist her in the realisation of the commission and publication. Our thanks go to them and to Nav Haq and Lucy Badrocke at Arnolfini and Suzanne Cotter and Emily Smith at Modern Art Oxford for organising the presentation of the work at their respective institutions and their ongoing contributions to the success of the series.

The 3 Series is made possible through Arts Council England's Grants for the Arts awards and we are particularly grateful to Arts Council South East for their adventurous support since the initial proposal. Valuable additional support for the production of Johanna Billing's work has been received from Iaspis and the Swedish Embassy, London.

JENNI LOMAX
DIRECTOR, CAMDEN ARTS CENTRE

TOM TREVOR
DIRECTOR, ARNOLFINI

MICHAEL STANLEY
DIRECTOR, MODERN ART OXFORD

JOHANNA BILLING

Born 1973 Jönköping, lives/works Enskede, Sweden

Education
1994–99 Konstfack International College of Arts, Crafts and Design, Stockholm

Solo Exhibitions
2010
I'm Lost Without Your Rhythm, Modern Art Oxford
2009*
I'm Lost Without Your Rhythm, Camden Arts Centre, London & Arnolfini, Bristol*
Taking Turns, Kemper Museum, Kansas City
2008
This Is How We Walk On The Moon, Malmö Konsthall, Malmö
This Is How We Walk On The Moon, Kavi Gupta Gallery, Chicago
2007
Forever Changes, Museum für Gegenwartskunst, Basel*
Keep on Doing, Dundee Contemporary Arts, Dundee
Silent Running, Raster, Warsaw
This Is How We Walk On The Moon, Collective Gallery, Edinburgh
Another Album and other films, Jönköpings Läns Museum, Jönköping
Stages: Another Album, Foundacio La Caixa, Barcelona*
Another Album, Hollybush Gardens, London
Magic & Loss and other films, Joan Prats Gallery, Barcelona
Magical World, Galeria Posibla, Bucharest
New Media Series: Johanna Billing, Saint Louis Art Museum, Saint Louis
2006
Songs, Cities & Circles, Basis, Frankfurt
Magical World, PS.1, New York
Magic & Loss, Kavi Gupta Gallery, Chicago
More films about Songs, Cities and Circles, Marabouparken, Stockholm
Magical World, Standard, Oslo
SubUrban: Johanna Billing, Knoxville Museum of Art, Knoxville*
2005
Magical World, Hollybush Gardens, London
2004
Look Out!, Kavi Gupta Gallery Project Room, Chicago
You Don't Love Me Yet, Vedanta Gallery, Chicago
2003
Studio Works, Milch at Gainsborough Studios, London
You Don't Love Me Yet, Index, Stockholm
2002
Where She Is At, Bild Museet, Umeå
2001
Where She Is At, Moderna Museet Projekt, Stockholm/Oslo Kunsthall, Oslo
Keep On Doing, Sub Bau, Gothenburg
2000
Project for a Revolution, Galleri Flach, Stockholm
1999
Coming Up, 149A, The Royal Academy of Art, Stockholm
1998
Straight from the Hip, Ynglingagatan 1, Stockholm
1996
Är du lik en känd person?, Galleri Service, Stockholm

Group Exhibitions
2009
Yebisu Int. Festival, Tokyo Metropolitan Museum of Photography, Tokyo
Sound of Music, Turner Contemporary Project Space, Margate
Stop.look.listen, Haggerty Museum of Art, Milwaukee
No more reality: crowd and performance, DEPO, Istanbul
A Letter Concerning Enthusiasm, AR/GE Kunst Galerie Museum, Bozen
Audio, Video, Disco, Kunsthalle Zürich, Zürich
2008
Periferic Biennal 8 – Art as Gift, Iasi, Romania
Here We Dance, Tate Modern, London
Amateurs, CCA Wattis, San Francisco
Spaport, Banja Luka, Bosnia and Herzegovina
Sonic Youth, Green on Red Gallery, Dublin
Terminus, Para/Site Art Space, Hong Kong
Muoviti fermo! I am sad to tell you, Centro per l'arte contemporanea Luigi Pecci, Prato
Held Together With Water, Istanbul Museum of Modern Art, Istanbul*
68-08, Färgfabriken, Stockholm

Tarantula, Trussardi Foundation, Milan
Ask a Banana Baby, Howard House Contemporary Art, Seattle
Something Must Break, OFF Festival, Mysłowice
Into the Music, Kunstraum München, München
Wollust – The presence of absence, Columbus Art Foundation, Leipzig
Protest und Widerstand im Eigensinn der Kunst, galerie 5020, Salzburg
TINA B, The Prague Contemporary Art Festival, Prague
Stutter & Twitch, Justina M. Barnicke Gallery, Toronto
Video salon 3, Curatorial Rebound Project, Galerija 10m^2, Sarajevo
Pop goes the Weasel, Badisher Kunstverein, Karlsruhe
Gravity in Art, Telic Arts Exchange, Los Angeles
Obscure, Sørlandet Art Museum, Kristiansand
Just Play – Music as Social Practice, Edith Russ site, Oldenburg
Gallery Jade at Galerie Diana Stigter, Amsterdam
Italia, ARCOS – Museo D'Arte Contemporanea del Sannio, Benevento
2007
Documenta 12, Kassel*
Playback, Musee d'Art Moderne, Paris
NUIT BLANCHE, First Baptist Church, Toronto
Black Is Black S.M.A.K, Ghent
Last Compositions at Amagerfaelledvej, Copenhagen
Intimacy, Ivan Dougherty Gallery, Paddington
Exploded View, Studio la Città, Verona
Stop. Look. Listen, Herbert F. Johnson Museum of Art, Ithaca
The Screen Eye of the New Image, Casino Luxembourg, Luxembourg*
Re-, Site Gallery, Sheffield
The Weasel: Pop Music and Contemporary Art, South London Gallery, London
Silence, Listen to the Show, Fondazione Sandretto Re Rebaudengo, Turin
Video-Salon 2, galerija 10m^2, Sarajevo
The Eventual, Frac Bourgogne, Dijon
Free Electrons, Lemaitre's video collection, tabacalera, International Contemporary Cultural Center of San Sebastián, San Sebastián
Held Together With Water, MAK, Vienna
Stutter and Twitch, CCS Bard, Annadale-on-Hudson
The Routines of Resistance, Standard, Oslo
Dreamlands Burn, Kunsthalle Budapest, Budapest
Sometime Waiting, Kadist Art Foundation, Paris
Confined Innocence, Artcite, Windsor, Canada
2006
Belief, Singapore Biennale, Singapore*
Try again, Fail Again, Fail Better, Momentum – 4th Nordic Festival of Contemporary Art, Moss*
I (Ich) Performative Ontology, Secession, Vienna
Here and now real, not yet concrete, Moderna Galerija, Ljubljana*
In a Magical World, Nit Niu 06, Cala Sant Vicens, Mallorca
Where She Is At, STUK, Leuven
No More Reality, Center For Cultural Decontamination, Belgrade*
Fantom, Charlottenborg Exhibition Hall, Copenhagen
Setting the Scene, Accademia di Belle Arti, Rome
Outside the Living Room, GB Agency, Paris
Leap into the cold water, Shedhalle, Zürich
Everyday Every other day, Blackwood Gallery, University of Toronto, Mississauga
Group Dynamics, Aspen Art Museum, Aspen
Don Quijote, Witte de With, Rotterdam
Normalisation, Rooseum Centre for Contemporary Art, Malmö
Biennial Cuvée, OK, Linz
2005
The Gravity in Art, De Appel, Amsterdam
Johanna Billing & Alan Currall, Display, Prague
Art that works / ***Catch Me***, 46th October Art Salon, Belgrade
Istanbul, 9th Istanbul Biennale, Istanbul*
Rock Music (dedicated to Igor Zabel), Gallery P74, Ljubljana
ADAM, Smart Project Space, Amsterdam
With or without?, Cultural Center, Belgrade
Blava Narrow Focus, Tranzit, Bratislava
Dialectics of Hope, 1st Moscow Biennale, Moscow*
Havlandet, The West Norway Museum of Decorative Art, Bergen
Do Not Interrupt your Activities, Royal College of Art, London*
New Art Event, Ulrich Museum of Art, Wichita, Kansas

Revolution is on hold, L'Associazione Isola dell'Arte, Milan
2004
Normalisation, Nova Gallery, Zagreb
Delayed on Time, Museum of Contemporary Art, Zagreb*
Collect Call, H.arta, Timisoara, Romania
The Yugoslav Biennial of Young Artists, Vrsac/Belgrade*
The Principle of Hope, Three Colts Gallery, London
Green Box, Trafo Gallery, Budapest
Pipshow #6, Fabrikken, Oslo
2003
The Edstrandska Foundation Prize, Malmö Konsthall, Malmö
Socialism - A Love Letter, Fia Backstrom, New York
The Peripheries Become The Center, Prague Biennale 1, Prague*
Delays and Revolutions, 50th International Venice Biennale, Venice*
Vinyl Sky, Intro,Vilnius
Kropp Idrott Konster, Blekinge Museum, Karlskrona
Perfect Performance, kulturhuset Stockholm
2002
Baltic Babel, Rooseum Center for Contemporary Art, Malmö
P_A_U_S_E, Gwangju Biennale, Gwangju*
Vårvideo, Kalmar Konstmuseum, Kalmar
2001
Projects for a Revolution, Le Mois de la photo à Montréal, Montreal*
The Path of Resistance, Moderna Museet, Stockholm*
Intentional Communities, Rooseum, Malmö; CAC, Vilnius
I'll Never Let You Go, Panacea Festival, Moderna Museet, Stockholm*
2000
Onufri "00" In and Out, National Gallery of Tirana*
Lost in Space, Färgfabriken, Stockholm*
My Generation, Kulturhuset, Stockholm
Viva Scanland, Catalyst Arts, Belfast
Swe.de, Rikstutställningar; Uppsala Konstmuseum; Sandvikens Konsthall; Jönköpings Museum; Röda Sten, Gothenburg
1999
Eslövs Julsaga, Eslöv
Light Show, Signal, Malmö
Dummy, Catalyst Arts, Belfast
1998
Index Edition Multiple Show, Index, Stockholm
Performance, An Art Brothel, Herkulesgatan, Stockholm

Selected Projects
2002-08
You Don't Love Me Yet, Film and live tour: Index, Stockholm, Eskilstuna Konstmuseum; Norrkopings Konstmuseum; Tingshuset Östersund; Frieze Art Fair, London; Vara Konserthus; Nifca, Helsinki; Sjömanskyrkan, Gävle; Ystad Konstmuseum; Vedanta Gallery, Chicago; Milton Keynes Gallery; *If I can't dance I don't want to be part of your revolution*, Festival a/d/ Werf, Utrecth; The Lab, San Francisco; Madrid Abierto, Madrid; Kammerspiele, Munich
2005
Makeover, What ever happened to Social Democracy?, Umeå Konsthögskola Project at Rooseum Center for Contemporary Art, Malmö
Happy Pappy, 'Do, Ut, Des; I give so that you may give', Publication, London
Pastor Bonus, Publication, Bogota/Oslo/Mexico
2004
Slim Volume, Poster Publication
Tranzit, Magazine Project, Respekt/der Standard in collaboration with Maria Crista

Grants and Residencies
2006
Swedish Arts Council Working Grant
2005
46th Oktober Art Salon, Award, Belgrade
West Balkan Air, Nifca Recidency, What, How and for Whom, Zagreb
2004
Stockholm Stad Kulturstipendium
2003
The Edstrandska Foundation Prize
2001
Swedish Arts Council Working Grant
1999
IASPIS International Artists' Studio Program in Sweden

* *Denotes publication*

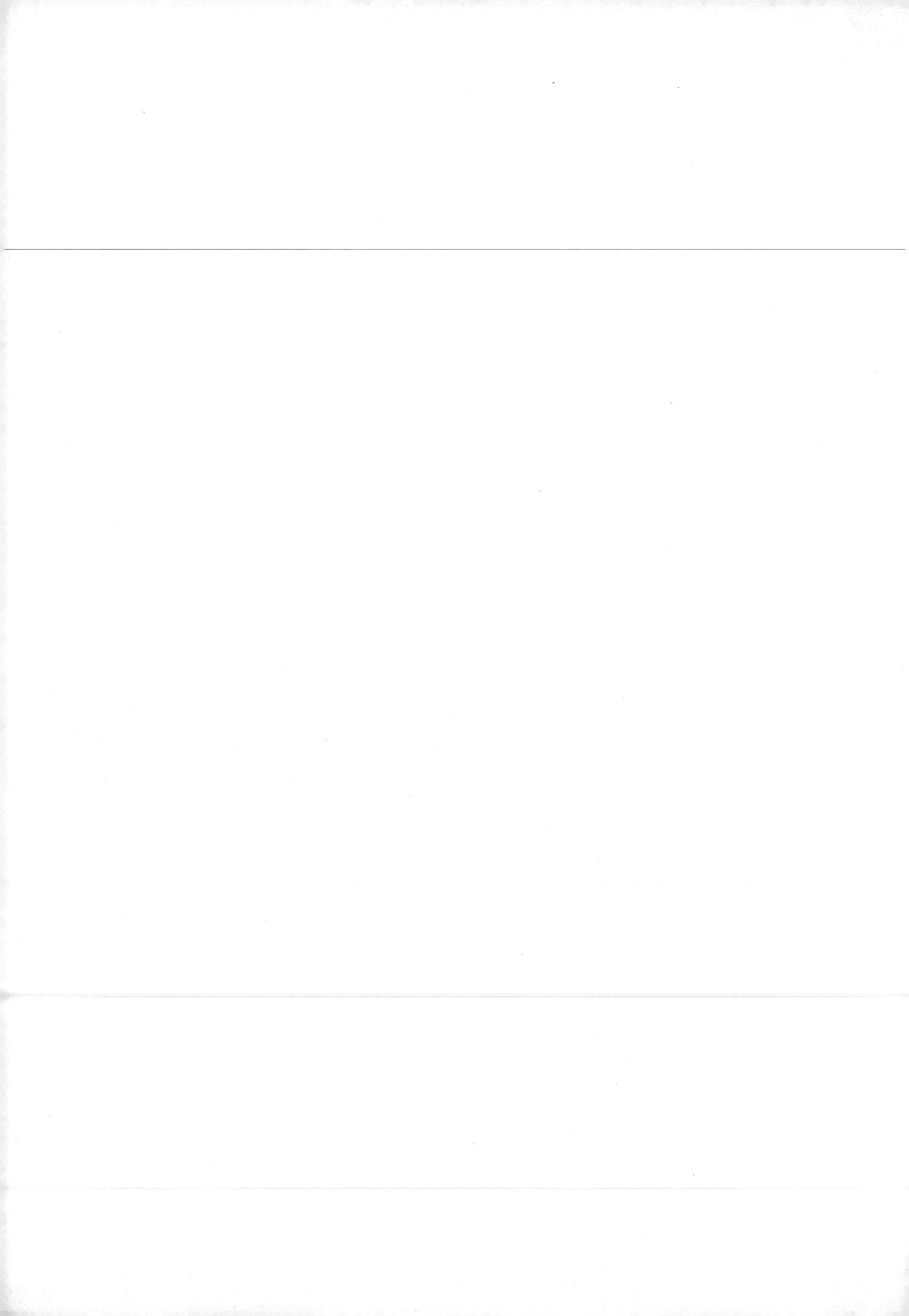

JOHANNA BILLING
I'M LOST WITHOUT YOUR RHYTHM

Published to accompany the exhibition
Johanna Billing *I'm Lost Without Your Rhythm*

10 July – 13 September 2009
Camden Arts Centre, Arkwright Road, London NW3 6DG
T. +44 (0)207 472 5500
www.camdenartscentre.org

12 September – 8 November 2009
Arnolfini, 16 Narrow Quay, Bristol, BS1 4QA
T. +44 (0)117 917 2300
www.arnolfini.org.uk

26 March – 23 May 2010
Modern Art Oxford, 30 Pembroke Street, Oxford, OX1 1BP
T. +44 (0)1865 722 733
www.modernartoxford.org.uk

Edited by Bruce Haines and Anne-Marie Watson
Designed by Secondary Modern (www.secmo.dircon.co.uk)

Printed by Lecturis, Eindhoven in an edition of 1000 copies

Distributed in the UK by
Art Data International, 12 Bell Industrial Estate,
50 Cunningham Street, London, W4 5HB, UK
T. +44 (0)2087471061; F. +44 (0) 2087422319

Photography: Lavinia German, except pages 2, 4, 13, 42, 50, 53, 63: Johanna Billing

ISBN 978 1 900470 94 0

Camden arts centre

MODERN ART OXFORD

ARNOLFINI

3 artists 3 spaces 3 years

is funded by the National Lottery through Arts Council England. Johanna Billing *I'm Lost Without Your Rhythm* is supported by the Embassy of Sweden.

I'm Lost Without Your Rhythm, live workshop/event at Casa di Studentilor, Iasi, 6-8 October 2008
I'm Lost Without Your Rhythm, 2009, a film by Johanna Billing

Choreography: Anna Vnuk
Cinematography: Manne Lindwall, Alexandru Grigoras, Johanna Billing
Sound: Paul Gradinariu
Still photographer: Lavinia German
Project coordinator: Alexandru Bonegru
Project assistants: Karl Jonas Winqvist
Assistants at Casa di studentilor: Adrian Poroh
Elvys Sandu Prisecaru

Featuring:
Bodănrescu Cristina, Denisa Pirţac, Florin Caracala, Sandra Prigoreanu, Laurenţiu Vasilache, Corneliu Laur, Bianca Buhă, Adrian Iacov, Oana Teodorescu, Monica Gavriluţă, Giana Mathaboya, Lucian Sîrbu, Alexandru Ignat

Live Musicians:
Drums and percussion: Theodor Popescu
Piano: Paul Pintile
Marimba and percussion: Cristina Lupu

Additional soundtrack recording:
My Heart (originally written by Mariam Wallentin and performed by Wildbirds and Peacedrums, 2008) performed by Per Lager (drums, vocals) Andreas Söderström (marimba, steeldrums, vocals), Pia Påltoft (vocals) Pernilla (vocals) Johanna Billing (vocals) Karl-Jonas Winqvist (vocals) produced by Johanna Billing, recorded and mixed by Tuomas Hakava, Up and Running studio, Stockholm. Mastered by Joachim Ekermann

Produced by Camden Arts Centre, London; Arnolfini, Bristol and Modern Art Oxford as part of the 3 Series: 3 artists, 3 spaces, 3 years, in the frame of Periferic 8 - Art as Gift, Biennial for Contemporary Art, Iasi, Romania with support from Iaspis, Sweden

Thanks to Theodor Popescu and the National Opera in Iasi for lending the marimba; Anticariatul Grumăzescu, Adrian Căliman at Casa di Stuentilor; Alexandru and Mircea Ignat at Qusar Dance; Alexandru Bonegru, Matei Benjaru, Dora Hegyi, Henry Moore Selder, Wildbirds & Peacedrums, Julian and Karl-Jonas Winqvist